Reading STREET
Grade K

Scott Foresman

Practice Book 4
Unit 4

© Pearson Education K

PEARSON
Scott Foresman

Editorial Offices: Glenview, Illinois • Parsippany, New Jersey • New York, New York
Sales Offices: Needham, Massachusetts • Duluth, Georgia • Glenview, Illinois
Coppell, Texas • Sacramento, California • Mesa, Arizona

ISBN: 0-328-14512-2

Copyright © Pearson Education, Inc.

All Rights Reserved. Printed in Mexico. This publication
is protected by Copyright, and permission should be obtained from the
publisher prior to any prohibited reproduction, storage in a retrieval
system, or transmission in any form by any means, electronic, mechanical,
photocopying, recording, or likewise. For information regarding permission(s),
write to: Permissions Department, Scott Foresman, 1900 East Lake Avenue,
Glenview, Illinois 60025.

25 V0B4 14

© Pearson Education K

Contents

Unit 4
Let's Explore

© Pearson Education K

Color pictures that begin with /h/.

© Pearson Education K

Family Times

You are your child's first teacher!

This week we're ...

Reading *Bunny Day*

Talking About Adventures

Learning About Connect /h/ to *Hh*
Sequence

Here are ways to help your child practice skills while having fun!

Day 1 — Read Together

Read the poem and help your child make a list of words that start with /h/.

> **Harry the heavy hippo**
> **had a huge house.**
> **He hid in the house**
> **afraid of a helpless mouse.**

Day 2 — Read Together

Have your child read the Phonics Story *I Have!* Find /h/ words.

Day 3 — Initial *Hh*

Write *hat, hop,* and *him* on paper. Have your child change the last letter in each word to make new words. Make a list of all the new words your child is able to make.

Day 4 — Naming Parts

Think of things in and around your home that start with *Hh*. Have your child identify and say the words while you make a list. For example, *hamper, high chair, hair dryer*.

Day 5 — Practice Handwriting

Have your child practice writing words that start with *Hh*.

hot   hit   him   hop   ham

Words to talk about

chores	tidy	bustle
race	story	hungry

Words to read

are	that	do
me	with	she
hop	hot	him
hat	hid	hit

© Pearson Education K

Name _____

✏️ Write   🖍️ Color

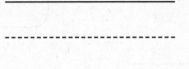 

Hh

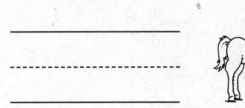

© Pearson Education K

Directions: Name the pictures. Write *h* on the line if the word begins with /h/. Color the /h/ pictures.

School + Home **Home Activity:** Have your child find other words with /h/ as in *hat*.

Name _____

 Write  Color

are	that	do

_____

_ _ _ _ _ _ _ _ _ _ _ _ _ _ _ _ _ _ _ _

_____ they little?

_____

_ _ _ _ _ _ _ _ _ _ _ _ _ _ _ _ _ _ _ _

_____ you like cats?

_____

_ _ _ _ _ _ _ _ _ _ _ _ _ _ _ _ _ _ _ _

We _____ little.

_____

_ _ _ _ _ _ _ _ _ _ _ _ _ _ _ _ _ _ _ _

_____ is a little hat.

 Directions: Write the missing word to finish each sentence. Color the pictures.

 Home Activity: Have your child use the high-frequency words in other sentences.

© Pearson Education K

I like my hat.

Do you like my hat?

4

Phonics Story *I Have!*
Target Skill Consonant *Hh*/h/

© Pearson Education K

I Have!

I have a hat.

The hat is little.

That is my hat.

The hat is on me.

It is my little hat.

Do you have a little hat?

2

I can hop with the hat.

I can hit with the hat.

© Pearson Education K

3

Name _____

 Number  Color

 Directions: Have children number the pictures to show what happened first, next, and last. Color the pictures.

 Home Activity: Have your child tell the steps to make something.

© Pearson Education K

Name _____

✏️ Write 🖍️ Color

_____
- - - - - - - - - - - - - - - -
_____

_____
- - - - - - - - - - - - - - - -
_____

_____
- - - - - - - - - - - - - - - -
_____

Hh

_____
- - - - - - - - - - - - - - - -
_____

_____
- - - - - - - - - - - - - - - -
_____

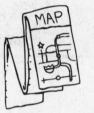

_____
- - - - - - - - - - - - - - - -
_____

 Directions: Name each picture. Write the letter for the beginning sound. Color the /h/ pictures.

 Home Activity: Have your child write rhyming /h/ words for these words: *cat, top,* and *sit.* Draw a picture for each word.

© Pearson Education K

8 **Phonics** Consonant *Hh*/h/

Practice Book Unit 4

Name _____

 Color

© Pearson Education K

 Directions: Have children color the picture that shows what comes first in each story.

School + Home **Home Activity:** Ask your child to draw three pictures to show how to make a sandwich.

Practice Book Unit 4

Comprehension Sequence **9**

Name _____

 Circle  Color

The cat can hit.

The bat hid on the top.

Hob can see the top.

A man sat on the mat.

Directions: Circle the naming part of each sentence. Color the naming part in the picture.

 Home Activity: Have your child make a new sentence using the naming part (subject) of each sentence.

Color pictures that begin with /l/.

Family Times

You are your child's first teacher!

This week we're ...

Reading *My Lucky Day*

Talking About Adventures

Learning About Connect /l/ to *Ll*
Cause and Effect

© Pearson Education K

Here are ways to help your child practice
skills while having fun!

Day 1 — **Read Together**

Read the following sentences and have your child identify the words that start with /l/: *Lil loves yellow lemons. Larry likes big lions.* Then help your child make other sentences.

Day 2 — **Read Together**

Have your child read the Phonics Story *Lad and Me.* Find /l/ words.

Day 3 — **Initial *Ll***

Write *la__* and *li__* on a sheet of paper. Have your child add letters to make words. Make a list of the words. Possible words are *lad, lap, lid, lip, lit.*

Day 4 — **Action Parts**

Have your child name some action words. Help him or her make a list of these words. Have your child use the words in sentences.

Day 5 — **Practice Handwriting**

Have your child practice writing words that have the sound /l/.

lap   lad   pill   fill   hill

Words to talk about

piglet	fox	lucky
filthy	cook	scrubber

Words to read

are	that	do
she	like	little
lad	lap	pill
hill	hat	lit

© Pearson Education K

Name _____

 Write Color

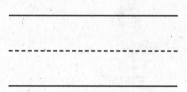

L l

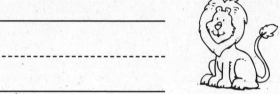

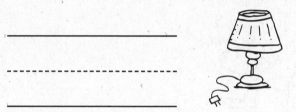

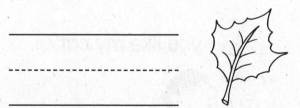

© Pearson Education K

Directions: Name each picture. Write *l* on the line if the word begins with /l/. Color the /l/ pictures.

 Home Activity: Find pictures that begin with /l/. Paste the pictures on paper to make a /l/ book.

Name _____

 Write ✏️ Color

$$\boxed{\text{do} \qquad \text{that} \qquad \text{are}}$$

_____

- - - - - - - - - - - - - - - - - -

_____ you see the man?

_____

- - - - - - - - - - - - - - - - - -

We _____ at the top.

_____

- - - - - - - - - - - - - - - - - -

Is _____ the lid?

_____

- - - - - - - - - - - - - - - - - -

_____ you like my cat?

🍎 **Directions:** Write the missing word to finish each sentence. Color the pictures.

 Home Activity: Have your child use the high-frequency words in other sentences.

14 **High-Frequency Words**

Practice Book Unit 4

© Pearson Education K

Lad can hop on the lid.

I can do that.

We are on the lid.

© Pearson Education K

Phonics Story *Lad and Me*
Target Skill Consonant *Ll/l/*

Lad and Me

Lad is my cat.

Lad is little.

Do you like Lad?

I like Lad.

Lad can sit in my lap.

Lad can sit a lot.

2

Lad can hop.

Lad can hop a lot.

I can do that.

© Pearson Education K

Name _____

 Draw

 Directions: Draw a line to match what happened with the picture that shows why it happened.

 Home Activity: Have your child draw a picture of something that makes him or her feel happy.

© Pearson Education K

Name _____

 Write  Color

_____
id
- - - - - - - - - - - - - - - - -

_____
mi
- - - - - - - - - - - - - - - - -

_____
hi
- - - - - - - - - - - - - - - - -

Ll

_____
ip
- - - - - - - - - - - - - - - - -

_____
ap
- - - - - - - - - - - - - - - - -

_____
fi
- - - - - - - - - - - - - - - - -

 Directions: Write *l* if the word begins with /l/. Write *ll* if the word ends with /l/. Color the pictures.

School + Home **Home Activity:** Have your child draw a picture of something that begins with /l/.

© Pearson Education K

Name _____

 Color

  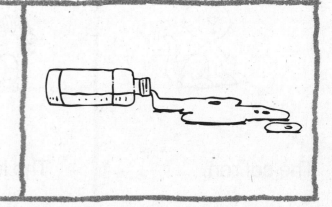

 Directions: Look at the first picture. Color the picture that tells why it happened.

 Home Activity: Show your child simple cause-and-effect relationships in your home (alarm clock ringing, phone ringing, someone knocking on door).

© Pearson Education K

Name _____

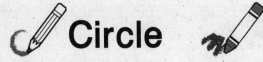 Circle  Color

The cat ran.

The lad hops.

The rat hid.

Nan taps.

 Directions: Circle the action part of the sentence and color the picture that shows the action.

 Home Activity: Help your child write simple sentences and find the action part.

© Pearson Education K

20 **Grammar** Action Parts in Sentences

Practice Book Unit 4

Color the pictures that begin with blends. Circle the pictures that end with blends.

Family Times

You are your child's first teacher!

This week we're ...

Reading *One Little Mouse*

ONE LITTLE MOUSE
by Dori Chaconas
illustrated by LeUyen Pham

Talking About   Animal Adventures

Learning About   Consonant Blends
Sequence

© Pearson Education K

4

1

Here are ways to help your child practice skills while having fun!

© Pearson Education K

Day 1 — Read Together

Say each pair of words and have your child tell which word has a blend: *Fran, ran; crib, rib; Sid, slid; cap, clap; pan, plan; dip, drip; stop, top; pot, spot; tap, trap; lip, flip.* Help your child make silly sentences with the words.

Day 2 — Read Together

Have your child read the Phonics Story *My Words*. Make a list of words with blends. Help your child use the words in sentences.

Day 3 — Blends

Have your child choose the word in each pair with the final consonant blend. Say these pairs: *sad, sand; dip, disk; mask, mat; mill, milk; raft, rat.*

Day 4 — Sentences

Have your child tell you the story *One Little Mouse* using complete sentences to tell about the events in the story.

Day 5 — Practice Handwriting

Have your child practice writing words with blends.

clap   drop   flat   stop

milk   band   fast   desk

Words to talk about

nest	woodland	vale
hollow	comfortable	shadows

Words to read

one	two	three
four	five	drip
clap	drop	milk

Name _____

✏ Write   ✏ Color

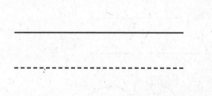

Directions: Name each picture. Write the blend for the beginning sound. Color the pictures.

School + Home **Home Activity:** Have your child point out initial consonant blends in the words in a book or magazine.

Practice Book Unit 4

Phonics Consonant Blends *sl-, pl-, cl-, fl-* **23**

© Pearson Education K

Name _____

 **Write**  **Color**

| one   two   three   four   five |

_____

- - - - - - - - - - - - - - - - - - -

I see _____ flags.

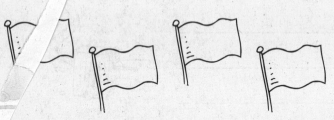

_____

- - - - - - - - - - - - - - - - - - -

I see _____ frogs.

_____

- - - - - - - - - - - - - - - - - - -

I see _____ rats.

_____

- - - - - - - - - - - - - - - - - - -

I see _____ clips.

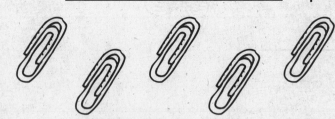

 Directions: Read each sentence. Have children write the missing word to finish each sentence and color the pictures.

 Home Activity: Have your child use *one, two, three, four,* and *five* in other sentences.

© Pearson Education K

I can tap.

Tap is like trap.

Do you see one trap?

4

© Pearson Education K

Name _____

My Words

I have one cap.

Cap is like clap.

Can you clap?

1

I see one cab.

Cab is like crab.

Can you see three?

I can see one pot.

Pot is like spot.

Do you see two?

2

3

© Pearson Education K

Name _____

 Draw  Color

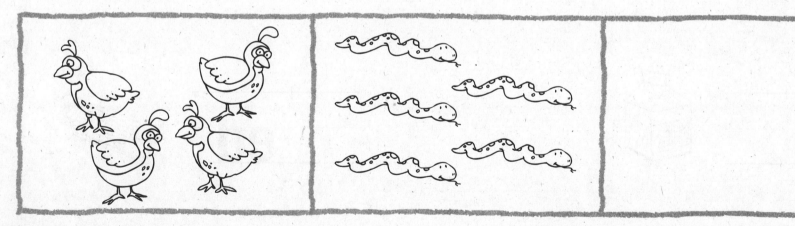

 Directions: Draw a picture to show which animal mouse met next. Draw the right number. Color the animals.

 Home Activity: Have your child draw a picture of the other animals the mouse met in the correct order.

Practice Book Unit 4

Comprehension Sequence **27**

Name _____

 Write  Color

_____
ba

_____
ne

_____
mi

_____
ib

_____
ill

_____
ed

 Directions: Write the letters for the consonant blends to finish each word. Color the pictures.

 Home Activity: Have your child use the words in sentences.

Practice Book Unit 4

Name _____

 Number

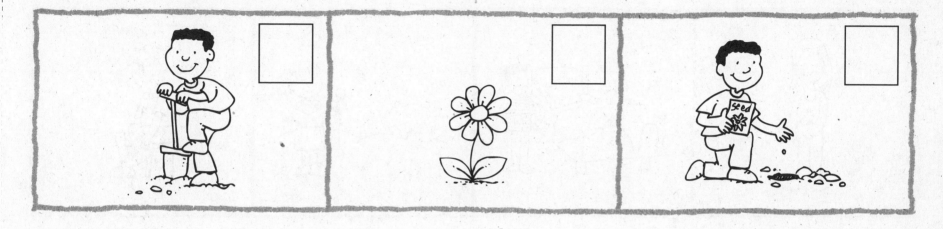

 Directions: Number the pictures to show what happened first, next, and last.

 Home Activity: Show your child how to cook a simple dish or make a craft.

© Pearson Education K

Name _____

 Draw  Color

© Pearson Education K

 Directions: Draw a line from the naming part to the correct action part. Color the pictures.

 Home Activity: Help your child write a complete sentence for the matching pictures.

Color the pictures that begin with /g/.

Family Times

You are your child's first teacher!

This week we're ...

Reading *Goldilocks and the Three Bears*

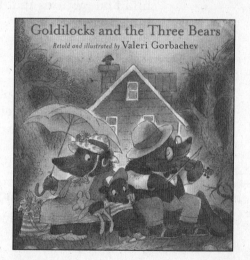

Talking About Adventures

Learning About Connect /g/ to *Gg*
Character

© Pearson Education K

Here are ways to help your child practice skills while having fun!

Day 1 **Read Together**

Have your child tell you the story of *Goldilocks and the Three Bears.* Then read a story to your child and ask questions about what happened first, next, and last.

Day 2 **Read Together**

Have your child read the Phonics Story *How Many?* Find the picture names that begin with /g/.

Day 3 **Connect *Gg* to /g/**

Look through a magazine or catalog and have your child find pictures that begin with /g/. Have your child circle each item.

Day 4 **Telling Sentences**

Write the following sentence on paper: *Bob can hop.* Read the sentence together. Ask who the sentence is about and what Bob can do. Then help your child write sentences about things he or she likes to do.

Day 5 **Practice Handwriting**

Have your child practice writing words that begin or end with *Gg.*

got   big   fog   dog   bag

Words to talk about

bears	porridge	cottage
big	middle-sized	small

Words to read

one	two	three
four	five	are
got	pig	get
dog	tag	dig

© Pearson Education K

2

3

Name _____

 Write   Color

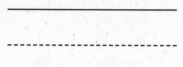

_____
- - - - - - - - - - - - - - - - -
_____

_____
- - - - - - - - - - - - - - - - -
_____

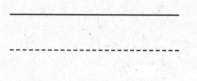

_____
- - - - - - - - - - - - - - - - -
_____

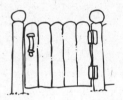

Gg

_____
- - - - - - - - - - - - - - - - -
_____

_____
- - - - - - - - - - - - - - - - -
_____

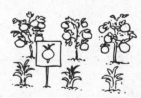

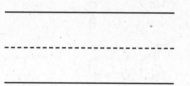
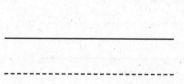

 Directions: Name each picture. Write *g* on the line if the word begins with /g/. Color the /g/ pictures.

 Home Activity: Find pictures that begin with /g/. Paste the pictures on paper to make a /g/ book.

© Pearson Education K

Name _____

 **Write** **Color**

one   two   three   four   five

_____

I can see _____ .

_____

I can see _____ .

_____

I can see _____ .

_____

I can see _____ .

 Directions: Write the missing word to finish each sentence. Color the pictures.

School + Home **Home Activity:** Have your child use the number words in sentences to tell about things in your home.

© Pearson Education K

Can you see four frogs?

Lin and Hap can see five frogs.

4

© Pearson Education K

Phonics Story *How Many?*
Target Skill Consonant *Gg*/g/

How Many?

Lin and Hap can see one dog.

I

Lin and Hap can see two kids.

Lin and Hap can see three pigs.

© Pearson Education K

Name _____

 Draw

© Pearson Education K

Directions: Have children tell a story about the
first box. Then draw the characters from the story
in each box.

 Home Activity: Ask your child to tell you about the
characters he or she drew.

Name _____

 Write  Color

oat

do

be

ate

le

ap

um

pi

 Directions: Write the letter to finish each word. Color the pictures that begin or end with /g/.

 School + Home **Home Activity:** Have your child name the pictures that begin with /g/.

© Pearson Education K

Name _____

 Color

 Directions: Look at the picture. Color the characters from *Goldilocks and the Three Bears* in the boxes.

School + Home **Home Activity:** Have your child tell about each character from the story.

© Pearson Education K

Name _____

 Draw  Color

The dog can nab it.	The pig is big.	The cat had one hat.	The log is little.

 Directions: Draw a line from the sentence to the picture it tells about. Color the pictures.

 Home Activity: Ask your child to tell you another sentence about each picture.

© Pearson Education K

Color the /e/ pictures.

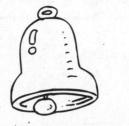

Family Times

You are your child's first teacher!

This week we're ...

Reading _If You Could Go to Antarctica_

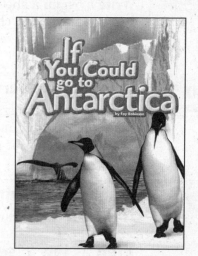

Talking About Antarctica Adventures

Learning About Connect /e/ to _Ee_
Classify and Categorize

© Pearson Education K

Here are ways to help your child practice skills while having fun!

Day 1 — Read Together

Read titles of stories and have your child tell what words have /e/: *The Little Red Hen, Green Eggs and Ham, Elves and the Shoemaker, Henny Penny,* and *The Enormous Egg.* Then read a story and look for /e/ words.

Day 2 — Read Together

Have your child read the Phonics Story *Ten, Ten, Ten!* Find and practice saying words with /e/.

Day 3 — Connect /e/ to *Ee*

Write *h__n* on a sheet of paper. Say the word *hen* and have your child write the missing letter. Continue with *pet, ten, met,* and *fed.*

Day 4 — Uppercase Letters and Periods

Look through a magazine with your child and have him or her point out uppercase letters. Also have your child point out periods at the end of sentences.

Day 5 — Practice Handwriting

Have your child practice writing short *e* words.

men   leg   set   get   pen

Words to talk about

Antarctica	**continent**	**icebergs**
penguins	**seals**	**whales**

Words to read

here	**go**	**from**
get	**let**	**pet**
net	**pen**	**hen**
men	**ten**	**fed**

© Pearson Education K

Name _____

 Color   Write

_____
- - - - - - - - - - - - - - -
_____

Ee

_____
- - - - - - - - - - - - - - -
_____

_____
- - - - - - - - - - - - - - -
_____

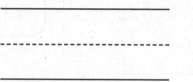

_____
- - - - - - - - - - - - - - -
_____

_____
- - - - - - - - - - - - - - -
_____

© Pearson Education K

 Directions: Name each picture. Write *e* on the line if the word begins with /e/. Color the /e/ pictures.

School + Home   **Home Activity:** Look through a newspaper or book with your child and point out words that begin with /e/.

Name _____

 **Write**  **Color**

| here | go | from |

_____
- -

Go _____ here to here.

_____
- -

We can _____ fast.

_____
- -

You can go _____ .

_____
- -

It is _____ me.

Directions: Write the missing word to finish each sentence. Color the pictures.

School + Home Home Activity: Have your child use the high-frequency words in other sentences.

© Pearson Education K

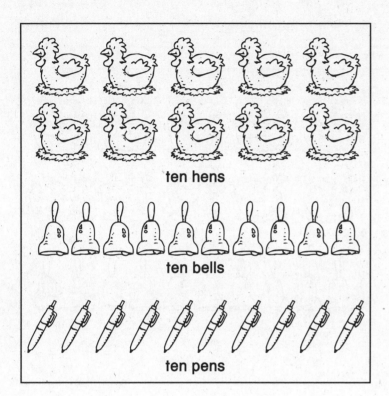

ten hens

ten bells

ten pens

I see ten, ten, ten!

4

Phonics Story *Ten, Ten, Ten!*
Target Skill Short *Ee*/e/

© Pearson Education K

Ten, Ten, Ten!

I have a pet hen.

Do you see my hen?

I can see ten.

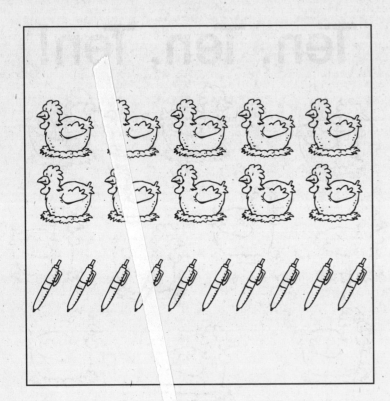

I have a fat pen.

Do you see my pen?

I can see ten.

2

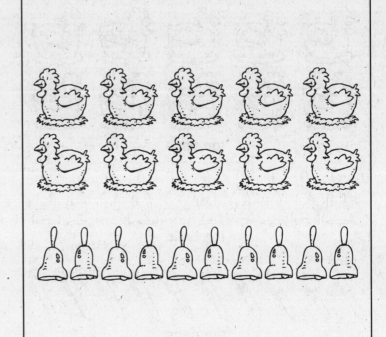

I have a red bell.

Do you see my bell?

I can see ten.

3

© Pearson Education K

Name _____

 Circle    Color

© Pearson Education K

 Directions: Circle items that belong together. Color those pictures in each row.

 Home Activity: Have your child draw three things that belong to the same group—toys, foods, or clothes.

Practice Book Unit 4

Comprehension Categorize and Classify **47**

Name _____

 **Write**   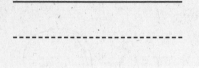 **Color**

_____
- - - - - - - - - - - -
_____

_____
- - - - - - - - - - - -
_____

_____
- - - - - - - - - - - -
_____

Ee

_____
- - - - - - - - - - - -
_____

_____
- - - - - - - - - - - -
_____

_____
- - - - - - - - - - - -
_____

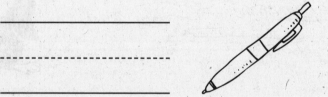

 Directions: Name each picture. Write the letter for the middle sound of each picture. Color the /e/ pictures.

School + Home **Home Activity:** Help your child make a list of words with /e/.

© Pearson Education K

Name _____

Circle **Color**

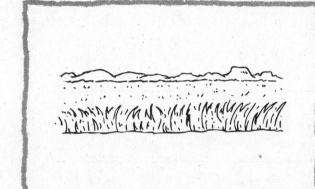

 Directions: Circle the pictures that belong together in each row. Color the pictures.

 Home Activity: Have your child tell why the pictures belong together.

Practice Book Unit 4

Comprehension Classify and Categorize **49**

© Pearson Education K

Name _____

 **Write**  **Draw**

the pet sat in a tent

_____

- -

_____

 Directions: Write the sentence using an uppercase letter and a period. Draw a picture for the sentence.

 Home Activity: Write sentences without uppercase letters and periods. Have your child write the sentences correctly.

© Pearson Education K

Family Times

You are your child's first teacher!

This week we're ...

Reading *Abuela*

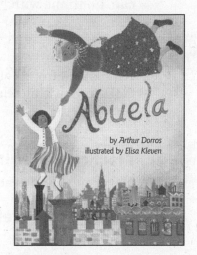

Talking About City Adventures

Learning About Connect /e/ to *Ee*
Setting

© Pearson Education K

Here are ways to help your child practice skills while having fun!

Day 1 | Read Together

Encourage your child to tell a story about a red elephant.

Day 2 | Read Together

Have your child read the Phonics Story *Ted and the Pet*. Find and practice saying words with /e/. Ask your child what the pet might be.

Day 3 | Using *Ee*

Write ___*ell* on a paper. Have your child add a letter to make as many rhyming words as he or she can. Continue with __*ed* and __*en*.

Day 4 | Pronoun *I*

Read aloud from a story book that uses the pronoun *I*. Have your child clap every time *I* is used in a sentence.

Day 5 | Practice Handwriting

Have your child practice writing words with /e/.

red   peg   tell   hen   sell

Words to talk about

abuela	adventure	flock
city	airport	harbor

Words to read

here	go	from
one	have	with
bed	leg	tell
well	men	set

© Pearson Education K

Name _____

 Write  Color

h n

m p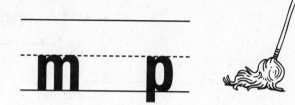

b d

Ee

p n

h t

n t

 Directions: Write *e*, *a*, or *o* to finish each word. Color the /e/ pictures.

School + Home **Home Activity:** Have your child write *pen* and *pan* and draw a picture for each word.

© Pearson Education K

Practice Book Unit 4

Phonics Short *Ee*/e/ **53**

Name _____

Abuela

 Write  Color

here   go   from

_____
- - - - - - - - - - - - - - - - - -
Did you _____ here?

_____
- - - - - - - - - - - - - - - - - -
I did not go _____.

_____
- - - - - - - - - - - - - - - - - -
I had to go _____ here to here.

_____
- - - - - - - - - - - - - - - - - -
I will _____ here.

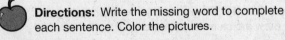 **Directions:** Write the missing word to complete each sentence. Color the pictures.

School + Home **Home Activity:** Have your child use the high-frequency words in other sentences.

© Pearson Education K

54 **High-Frequency Words**

Practice Book Unit 4

You can see the tent.

You can see the nest.

I have a pet.

Phonics Story *Ted and the Pet*
Target Skill Short *Ee*/e/

© Pearson Education K

Ted and the Pet

I am Ted.

I have a pet.

My pet is big.

I met my pet here.

My pet is in the tent.

It is a big tent.

2

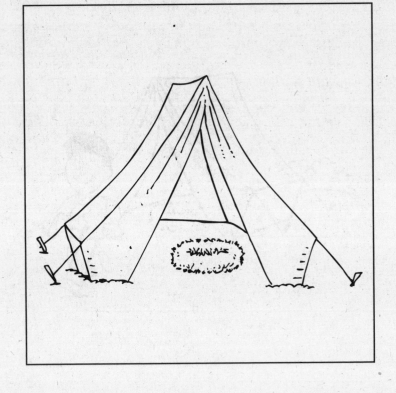

My pet can go to the tent.

My pet has a nest in the tent.

It is a big nest.

3

© Pearson Education K

 Draw  Color

 Directions: Draw a picture that tells where and when the story in the last box happened. Color the pictures.

 Home Activity: Draw a picture of where and when one of your favorite stories happened.

© Pearson Education K

Name _____

Circle ## Color

bed bad		bet bat	
log leg		pen pan	

Directions: Circle the word that names the picture.
Color the /e/ pictures.

School + Home **Home Activity:** Have your child draw a picture of something with /e/.

© Pearson Education K

Name _____

 Draw   Write

© Pearson Education K

 Directions: Draw your favorite scene from *Abuela*.
Then write or dictate words describing where and
when it happened.

 Home Activity: Talk about a favorite event with your
child. Discuss where and when it happened.

Practice Book Unit 4

Comprehension Setting **59**

Name _____

✏️ Draw

I am Ned.

I am Nell.

I am Meg.

I am Ken.

Directions: Draw lines connecting each child to his or her picture.

School + Home **Home Activity:** Ask your child to use the pronoun *I* in sentences.

© Pearson Education K